THE LATE POEMS OF MENG CHIAO

THE LOCKERT LIBRARY OF POETRY IN TRANSLATION

Editorial Advisor: Richard Howard
For other titles in the Lockert Library
see page 85

THE LATE POEMS OF

Meng Chiao

Translated by
David Hinton

Princeton University Press, Princeton, New Jersey

Copyright © 1996 by Princeton University Press
Published by Princeton University Press, 41 William Street,
Princeton, New Jersey 08540
In the United Kingdom: Princeton University Press, Chichester,
West Sussex

Library of Congress Cataloging-in-Publication Data

Meng, Chiao, 751–814.
[Poems. English. Selections]
The late poems of Meng Chiao / translated by David Hinton
p.   cm. — (Lockert library of poetry in translation)
Includes bibliographical references.
ISBN 0-691-01237-7 (alk. paper).
ISBN 0-691-01236-9 (pbk. : alk. paper)
1. Meng, Chiao, 751–814—Translations into English.
I. Hinton, David, 1954–   .   II. Title.   III. Series.
PL2677.M4A24   1997
895.1'13—dc20   96-21157

This book has been composed in Garamond with Optima display

Princeton University Press Books are printed on
acid-free paper and meet the guidelines for
permanence and durability of the Committee on
Production Guidelines for Book Longevity of
the Council on Library Resources

Printed in the United States of America
by Princeton Academic Press

10 9 8 7 6 5 4 3 2 1
10 9 8 7 6 5 4 3 2 1
(Pbk.)

The Lockert Library of Poetry in Translation
is supported by a bequest from
Charles Lacy Lockert (1888–1974)

Other Translations by
David Hinton

Chuang Tzu: Inner Chapters
The Selected Poems of Li Po
Landscape over Zero, poems by Bei Dao
Forms of Distance, poems by Bei Dao
The Selected Poems of T'ao Ch'ien
The Selected Poems of Tu Fu

CONTENTS

ACKNOWLEDGMENTS

Some of these poems first appeared in *SULFUR*.

The translation of this book was supported by
grants from the Ingram Merrill Foundation and
the National Endowment for the Arts.

INTRODUCTION

There is a black side to the profound sense of dwelling that grounds Chinese culture, and Meng Chiao is perhaps its consummate poetic master. Our belonging to the earth's natural processes has always been the primary source of spiritual affirmation in China's positivist culture, but it also means belonging to the consuming forces that drive those processes. Meng Chiao was imbued with the two great traditions of spiritual affirmation in China: Taoism, the ancient wellspring of Chinese spirituality, and Ch'an Buddhism (Zen), which was widely influential among the intellectual class during the T'ang and Sung dynasties. But while the Taoist/Ch'an worldview allows most great Chinese poets to inhabit the vulnerability of being human as a profoundly rich experience, Meng Chiao inhabits the consuming shadows of this vulnerability.

In voicing his singular poetic world, Meng creates a singular language. The use of objective imagery to express subjective states is an ancient convention in Chinese poetry, and the balance between objective and subjective is essential to the wisdom in nearly all its great poetry. But in Meng Chiao's bleak introspection, the balance tips heavily toward the subjective. He infuses this imagist poetics with such intensity that the images often become surreal in a uniquely Chinese way, and the poem as a whole often takes on symbolist dimensions able to express what conventional language cannot articulate. And this, in turn, affords him new depths of insight into the objective world. At its limits, as in "Laments of the Gorges," it is a language capable of articulating that murderous furnace at the heart of change.

Meng Chiao lived in truly desperate times. The illustrious T'ang Dynasty was foundering badly as a result of the An Lu-shan rebellion (755–63) and the chronic militarism it spawned. Of the country's 53 million people, the rebellion left 36 million either dead or displaced and homeless. The central government was crippled by factionalism and palace intrigue, and fighting off external threats continued to weaken it, while vast outlying regions were lost. At the same time, large areas of China itself splintered into dozens of semiautonomous regions ruled by warlords having no loyalty to the emperor, and the fighting between these warlords and the central government devastated the populace through unmanageable taxation, heavy conscription, and the widespread destruction of battle. Meanwhile, the empire's chaotic fragmentation continued until a massive peasant rebellion finally led to the T'ang's collapse in 907.

This desperate situation is everywhere in Meng Chiao's work. It appears in Meng's literal descriptions of his world, but more importantly, it is often internalized and transformed into an atmospherics of loss and disorientation. "Laments of the Gorges," for instance, can be read as a majestic elegy for the age's innumerable victims (especially devoted scholar-officials who died in unjust exile). This political engagement gives an added dimension to the achievement of Meng Chiao's experimental poetics.

Born in 751, Meng Chiao lived in the south as something of a poet-recluse until 791. He then went north to the capital, Ch'ang-an, to prepare for the national examinations, which would qualify him for a government position. In the south, he had associated with the literary circle of the Ch'an poet-monk Chiao-jan, and upon moving to the capital he met Han Yü, the great literary figure who was to become his close friend and ally. After failing twice, Meng passed the examination in 795, but no position was offered him. He traveled and lived in a number of places during the next five years, including two years in Pien-chou with Han Yü. Meng finally recieved a minor provincial position in 800. He was apparently so preoccupied with his literary pursuits that someone else soon had to take over his responsibilities, but he remained in this position at half-pay until 806, when he returned to Ch'ang-an.

Although it contains hints of the innovations that distinguish his late poetry, Meng Chiao's work to this point was decidedly mediocre: conventional verse often mired in petty obsessions and inevitably undone by his penchant for the strange and surprising. However, once Meng was reunited with Han Yü in the capital, his poetics began the remarkable transformation that led to his late work. At the end of 806, Meng moved to Lo-yang, the eastern capital of the empire, where he secured the patronage of the provincial governor. Han Yü arrived a year later, and together they cultivated an experimental poetics of startling disorientations. Han Yü returned to Ch'ang-an in 811, whereupon he returned to a more conventional poetics. Meng Chiao, on the other hand, remained in Lo-yang until his death in 814. It was during these years in Lo-yang, from 807 to 814, that he wrote the large sequences which are translated in this volume. This is truly major work, work which may be the most experimental in the tradition.

Meng Chiao's late poetry is an expansive and powerfully original extension of the formal possibilities Tu Fu (712–770) initiated in his late poetry: symbolist poetics, thick linguistic density and ambiguity, and the lyric sequence as an interrelated series of lyrics that form a single long poem. Tu Fu's influence is clear in terms of content as well. Though it hardly ignores life's hardships, the Chinese tradition is grounded in a poetry of balanced affirmation, its great poets speaking primarily of their immediate experience in a natural voice. The dark extremities of Tu Fu's late work extended this tradition to its limit, and Meng Chiao's stark introspective depths mark a clear break. Together with Han Yü, whose poetry in this mode is less accomplished and radical than Meng Chiao's, Meng opened an imaginative space so original it began an alternative tradition, a tradition which included a number of major poets, and at least two great ones: Li Ho and Li Shang-yin. But while these younger poets favored a dreamlike hermeticism, Meng always maintained a hard-edged immediacy and existential relevance.

The vitality of this movement proved rather short-lived, however, ending with Li Shang-yin's death in 858, although its preoccupations remained dominant for another century. While Meng Chiao and his heirs were working out the obsessive logic of their poetics, the tradition's mainstream continued to develop in the work of such poets as Po Chü-i. Deeply influenced by Ch'an, he practiced a poetics of social commitment, everyday human concerns, and clear plain-spoken language: a poetics which proved more enduring than the experimental alternative. And the Han Yü who wrote a simple and "unliterary" poetry was seen to be more important than the Han Yü who was Meng Chiao's literary ally in Lo-yang. The alternative tradition of Meng Chiao and his heirs made the Mid-T'ang (766–835) an especially rich poetic period, rivaling even its predesessor, the illustrious High T'ang (712–760), during which Chinese poetry reached its highest level of achievement in the work of Wang Wei, Li Po, and Tu Fu. But it was largely through the influence of the more conventional Mid-T'ang poets that the tradition's mainstream was passed on to the next great period of Chinese poetry: the Sung Dynasty, a period in which Ch'an's widespread influence led to a profoundly simple poetry of things at hand. Although Meng Chiao was very highly regarded for the first two centuries after his death, the Sung poets decried his bleak world and clotted language. Because the Sung poets answered so deeply to the Chinese sensibility, they came to have a defining influence on the Chinese tradition, and Meng was henceforth relegated to the status of a third-rank poet.

Quite unlike his kindred spirits who cultivate the ruins of solipsism in our modern western traditon, Meng Chiao employs quasi-surreal and symbolist techniques to explore the experience of being an integral part of the organic universe, and this sense of integration gives his fearful vision a kind of balance and deeper truth. Even so, his bleak world hardly answered to the Chinese expectation that great poetry embody a profound and affirming wisdom. Recently, however, there has emerged a new appreciation of Meng's work, not least because his innovations anticipated landmark developments in the modern western tradition by a millenium.

THE LATE POEMS OF MENG CHIAO

MOURNING LU YIN

1

Invariably pure and austere, poets mostly
starve to death embracing empty mountains,

and when white clouds have no master,
they just drift off, idle thoughts carefree.

Servants too weak to make arrangements
after a long illness, your body lies waiting

among all those prize books hungry mice
shredded and scattered through the house.

You've gone to the village of new ghosts
now. I look into a face white as old jade,

then watch your burial, ashamed no one
follows, clutching at you, calling you back.

At dusk, springs mourn by the hundred,
their empty lament flowing and flowing.

2

Hush of a loom's shuttle over and over,
one moon lights a thousand forevers

gone. All purity fresh again and again,
one spring blossoms a thousand forevers

gone, forever gone. Graveyard winds
my lament, Sung Mountain autumn's

now your tomb. And everywhere here,
all dust and dirt, graveyard guests

mourn, thorns and brambles voicing
bitter grief born of tear-soaked roots.

Where even fire couldn't warm itself,
the body's force fails quickly. Silent,

alone, I offer a cup of tears, start it
toward the clear Lo River, adding this

heart-stricken cry to that never-ending
sound of death dragging people apart.

3

Thorn-bramble winds keep calling out,
splintering all that bitter lament apart,

bitter lament no one could bear. You
cover your ears, but it keeps coming,

chords of sorrow, so many searing cries
over such lavish loss. The spirit's charred

mourning poverty, and mourning death
fires the heart to sheer ash. A moment's

shimmering dream, the world drifts deep
eddies of swelling tears. Burial songs

sung once, you're gone. And once weeds
close you in, they'll never open again.

4

At your home, deep grasses and trees
keeping roads narrow, sun and moon

no longer lavish you with their light.
Now, lichens clothe you for nothing.

It's all too sad. An old, childless man,
ants climbing across diseased flesh,

you'll just lie there year after year,
water's dark lament flowing, flowing,

dark lament tigers and leopards hear.
No one else comes to visit you now.

Poetry's the only family you've had,
and death's brought you home here.

For your elegy, Han Yü relies on you:
he makes an inkstick of these canyons

and grinds it into ink that lets words
shine through a thousand forevers.

5

Accounts never balance out for the noble:
life's bitter, and praise after death hollow.

Some endow sons and grandsons with their
renown; now yours endows mud and sand.

It's too sad – and your thousand poems lit
blossoms vanishing in a single morning:

bitter, hard-wrought words scattering away,
lament startling and empty wherever I go.

6

I hear an ancient sage of backalleys,
see that spare Lu Mountain recluse:

dying hungry, they gained renown,
renown in hunger like vast spring

mist. But for a simple old man, youth
fading, it seems a cloud of sorrow,

sorrow that's always this one grief:
It blurs us and the ancients together.

We'd always spoken of this. And now
you're so agreeable, we talk and talk.

7

When we met, our hair was lacquer black,
and we struggled to make language new.

We spent nights out on moonlit bridges,
or at some inn drinking on a bed, both

drunk after only two cups. Our fame
already spreading through the country,

we'd go picking plum blossoms at temples,
cut fleeting flowers in gardens. Desires

pure, we dined on green vegetable broths,
all interest in plump, juicy lamb gone,

or chanted poems, every rhyme crystal
clear, words full of ancient heartsong.

And then our hair was suddenly white,
those years of fullness a stolen promise.

Never seeking the muddy or the clear,
how could we accuse this river of fate?

8

Sages of old drank mourning-wine aplenty:
mourning-wine quiets a mourning heart,

and when sages later on tried giving it up,
they found their grief grown bottomless.

Youth is the season for mourning-wine,
that onslaught of white hair beginning,

and old age, too, is mourning-wine season,
each sound and echo like life and death.

If you send word to mourning-wine guests,
don't send Lu Yin's song. Lu Yin's empty

voice just drifted away – nowhere in all
heaven and earth, nowhere to be found.

9

Though few of our fellow humans grieve,
the birds and beasts all call out in sorrow,

and however senseless they seem at first,
they've reached into the depths of heaven.

No child means no tears when you sicken,
no father no one to suffer your memories.

Why separate family from everyone else?
To do it, people use the rites like a knife,

so you died alone, buried without mourners.
I kept lament to myself, hid this worry,

and let other hands lift you into the grave.
How can I praise your devotion now, your

sincerity? Lost, lost – a childless old man
like another feather lost among the molt.

10

Celestial immortals mourn such a sage –
bones transformed, spirit become stars,

your poems all rising through heaven,
sharpening constellations into bright

clarities. Like the rarest ancient poems,
yours are pure spirit. We call ethereal

poets of renown *banished immortals*,
ascending and descending without end,

for in poems we're made pure by death,
and without them we live mean lives.

Struck metal's the perfect song for you,
song bequeathed all repose down all time.

COLD CREEK

1

Frost rinsing water free of color, delicate
scales appear in Cold Creek. Come to this

hollow mirror of emptiness with delight,
I find a spent and sullen body shining back

there. Unable to hide itself now, something
prowling at bottom reappears – new again,

shimmering. Clear and open as the noblest
affections, this stream's a trap set for us.

Grown bright again, simple and shallow,
its heart frozen by night already flows full

this morning. And one handful, all emerald
clarity, rinses dust of a thousand worries

far away. Once footsteps muddy this water,
it's nothing like a pure mountain stream.

2

The Way flowing along these Lo-yang
shores is a creek fronting my ancestral

village. Pale ice passing boats shatter
clatters like blue agate. Green water

freezes into green jasper, whitewater
blossoming into emblems of white jade.

Setting this priceless mirror ablaze,
heaven's light evens all things out:

climbing down to its snaking menace,
clutching dead wood, I hear widows

crying. Frost, too, leaving spring scents
faint, evens out these frozen reaches.

Losing the path, I sit like some fool,
just watching and listening. Children

work, hoe brambles along the shore,
talk sorrow, sorrow, and more sorrow.

3

I sip wine at dawn, then cross the snow
out to this clear creek. Frozen into knife-

blades, rapids have sliced ducks open,
hacked geese apart. Stopping overnight

here left their feathers scattered, their
blood gurgling down into mud and sand.

I stand alone, dazed, words giving way
to that acrid clamor of the heart. Frozen

blood mustn't beget spring. If it begets
spring, newborn life's never evened out,

and if frozen blood breaks into blossom,
widow-tears begin. What isolate beauty:

a village all thorns and brambles, fields
all frozen and dead no one could plow.

4

Men pole boats, banking jade stars aside,
trailing out scattered fireflies. And cold

north plunging icy lament deep, starved
hunters chant invocations to hidden fish.

Frozen teeth gnaw and grind at themselves.
Windchimes clatter in sour wind. All this

immaculate grief – it's inescapable. It
rinses hearing clean of the least sound.

The current of rippling emerald is gone,
and colorful floss fallen, flight-tattered.

Ground glare ice, branches splintered,
things can't walk, can't roost. Wounded,

they squawk and shriek, yelp and howl,
accusing heaven: *will things ever rest?*

5

Water snakes then flows straight: scales,
how its bone-white dragon scales ripple,

frozen gusts tearing splintered confusion,
opening a bitter valley's minced and salted

wail. Our scribbling a feckless stammer,
birds and beasts care for us even more.

Our savage bowstrings broken, they come
fighting to the last gasp to be our guests.

All this austerity brings earth's routine
workaday killing to an end. Clarity, all one

shimmering ache of clarity – it's here that
source of change stirs, that life-bringing

promise: Clearing skies rinse sun and moon
clean. Planets and stars appear in azure

depths. But standing alone in the snow,
I chant for a thousand worries renewed.

Heaven's Aspersion Star blazes for nothing,
and Tongue Star rails on and on, empty.

Even sage Emperor Yao couldn't hear you.
Confucius took advice, but he was no one.

This invocation's written and fallen silent,
and still no trace of those ancient truths.

6

The dead froze. You can still eat them,
but killing winds haven't died down yet.

If we make loving-kindness a weapon,
loving-kindness lives at knife-point,

and at knife-point, loving-kindness
reeks. Where's the nobility in that?

Rising waves unsheathe swords of ice,
slash each other like enemies, bitter

enemies. Snow needling in, fish hearts
blush into brilliant reds, and it seems

some seething along shadowy edges
tells how it's been cut and sliced apart.

Ch'i born of some strange place – who
drove it into waters of our homeland,

cutting spring's first month all apart,
sealing darkness in a hundred valleys?

I gaze into clear skies, fresh sunlight
filling this grief and sorrow with doubt.

7

Bitter cold, the old man of the creek
weeps, frozen tears falling, a tinkling

clatter. Taking the form of birds dead,
beasts dead, snow slices a flurried heart.

Once frozen, a sword's edge won't cut,
and no one pulls bowstrings back now.

They say the valiant never eat heaven's
slaughter. Chopping down into jade,

I bury meat and bones, grief-stricken
sight itself a lament for all that beauty.

8

Windblown, last ice shudders on the creek,
creek holding the land's bright spring.

Blossoms drip and drip and drip. Jade melts,
setting the newborn dragon loose, scales

glittering into rippling curves clear. Spring
thaw begun, I bathe in these scented waters,

distant, a thousand miles of ice split open,
kind-hearted warmth in every ladleful.

Frozen spirits rinsing each other clean,
trickles struggle into life and flow anew.

Suddenly, as if all sword wounds were over,
the body of a hundred battles begins rising.

LAMENTS OF THE GORGES

1

Long ago, everyone laughed together,
but who's left to share this lament now,

lament of the gorges shadowy spirits
mourning. Winds howl. Sinking ghosts

embrace an empty moon, disappearing,
appearing – they can't stop themselves.

Pounding us to dust in a lightning flash,
spring's thundering thousand-foot swells

flood these gorges with sound, dragging
jade-pure currents through whirlpool

clarities. Riverbanks battered and awash,
sawtooth waves open. Snarling, snarling

and gaping bottomless, a swilling lure,
they promise unfathomed catastrophe,

spewing out the valley's brimful cries,
swirling embattled around rock's fury.

Long ago, they sent felons back home.
Now this prison's taking so many of us,

orphaned words empty resemblances,
each mouthful of snow startling still.

People shabby and low, true hearts few,
it's money makes friends. Yellow gold

buys you mourners. They've soon gone
home, though, their tears already dry.

But I mind the heart's old ways: for you,
emptiness broken and scattered away.

2

Water all heaven-above heaven-below,
a boat leaves earth entering earth here.

Swordblades of rock slice at each other,
rock-broken waves all angry dragons,

and though blossoms rekindle spring,
freezing winds make autumn timeless.

Unearthly voices rise from hidden dens.
Flies thicken, buzzing currents in flight.

The sun sunk deep, drowning lament,
how could we set out pleading for help?

3

Three Gorges one thread of heaven over
ten thousand cascading thongs of water,

slivers of sun and moon sheering away
above, and wild swells walled-in below,

splintered spirits glisten, a few glints
frozen how many hundred years in dark

gorges midday light never finds, gorges
hungry froth fills with peril. Rotting

coffins locked into tree roots, isolate
bones twist and sway, dangling free,

and grieving frost roosts in branches,
keeping lament's dark, distant harmony

fresh. Exile, tattered heart all scattered
away, you'll simmer in seething flame

here, your life like fine-spun thread,
its road a trace of string traveled away.

Offer tears to mourn the water-ghosts,
and water-ghosts take them, glimmering.

4

Young clear-voiced dragons in these
gorges howl. Fresh scales born of rock,

they spew froth of fetid rain, breath
heaving, churning up black sinkholes.

Strange new lights glint, and hungry
swords await. This venerable old maw

still hasn't eaten its fill. Ageless teeth
cry a fury of cliffs, cascades gnawing

through these three gorges, gorges
full of jostling and snarling, snarling.

5

In gorges, dragons voice age-old explanations.
In pools ten hundred feet deep, you hear them.

Cruel waves keep strict accounts, drinking
blood to nurture children and grandchildren,

but without ancient Kao Yao's gentle justice,
feasting on prison-drowned spirits is empty.

Something there, mystery haunting darkness,
the futile talk of ghosts goes on and ever on,

gorges hearing cascades cry lament, gorges
mourning widowed gibbons. There's nothing

human in the sound of gorges, gorges where
blades of churning water slice at themselves,

and now, sage hearts all hidden away here,
who marshals these bitter and drowned pleas?

6

These gorges a dragon's heart of lies,
loudmouth banks thirsty for accusation,

there's nothing honest in this feeding,
this voice brimful of such rank noise.

Rock teeth chewing a hundred streams,
rock winds singing a thousand *ch'in,*

you can't stay free of its isolate lament,
can't sort through this crack in snow.

Majestic spirit drifts high in the moon,
but deep in the clarity of gorges, dragon

dens endure. You can't embrace its pain,
and our pleas never shine clear. Empty

swordblades, flying billows and swells
carve a thousand peaks from solid rock.

7

Upper edges of these gorges shattering
sun and moon, sun and moon altogether

splintered light, things grow all tilted
away here, and birds tilt away in flight.

Hidden rocks locking teeth, summoned
spirits never return from these depths.

Wild flurries of armor, clear streams
clothe jade-pure rock in shimmering

color. And hungrily swallowed cascades
thunder, frothing like swirling grease.

You can't wander spring gorges: fetid
grasses already spread such lean stains.

8

Light flowing in gorges plays across cliffs,
shapes changing, blossoms spectral without

spring. Hidden among roots, jade-pure rain
gracing river crossings, froth blazes red.

This canyon dragon-hearted, river demons
people villages. Feeding on whatever lives,

they don't care if you're noble and wise.
We all nurse our lives into death alone,

nothing to trust among all our fetid words,
songs forced, happiness a sham. Unearthly

crops missing, fields tilt away, and savage
scales fill these poison waters. You can't

make such unearthly things friends, can't
work out lament in laments of the gorges.

9

Water swords and spears raging in gorges,
boats drift across heaving thunder. Here

in the hands of these serpents and snakes,
you face everyday frenzies of wind and rain,

and how many fleeing exiles travel these
gorges, gorges rank inhabitants people?

You won't find a heart beneath this sheen,
this flood that's stored away aftermath

forever. Arid froth raising boundless mist,
froth all ablaze and snarling, snarling –

what of that thirst for wisdom when you're
suddenly here, dead center in these waters?

10

Death-owls call in human voices. Dragons
wolf down heaving mountain waters. Here

in broad daylight, with all the enticing
serenity of a clear and breezy sky, they

beggar wisdom, snarling everything alive
in fetid gatherings of vine-covered depths.

Want filling fanged cascades bottomless,
sawtooth froth swells everywhere. Nesting

birds can't settle in trees tilted so askew,
trees gibbons leaping and swinging fill.

Who can welcome laments of the gorges,
gorges saying *What will come will come.*

APRICOTS DIED YOUNG

Apricots died young in blossoms still nipples.
Frost cut them free, and their scattering made me
mourn the child I had long ago,
so I wrote this poem.

1

Don't fondle these pearls. O hands of ice,
fondle pearls and they're quick to fly.

And don't cut spring short, sudden frost.
Cut spring and that blaze of beauty's lost.

Still nipples, tiny blossoms fall in tatters
tinged pure as a child's robes long ago.

I gather them, never filling my hands,
and at dusk, grief empty, return home.

2

Picking stars off the ground empty,
no blossoms left to gaze at in trees,

it's all grief and sorrow: a lone old
man grief, a childless home sorrow.

We're nothing like plunging ducks,
or crows gathering twigs for a nest:

wave-battered ducklings fly easily,
and little crows call proudly in wind.

Blossom and child won't come back.
In a world emptying grief, I mourn.

3

It must be this same thread of tears
piercing the hearts of spring trees:

before blossoms opened anywhere,
flake after flake fell to the blade.

Spring's life never lasts, it's true,
but my lament over frost is already

impossibly deep. Instead of blossoms
bathing streams, tears bathe robes.

4

At our son's birth, the moon was dark,
and when he died, it began to shine.

Moon and child, they stole each other
away. O scarcely lived child of mine,

what's it like, blossom after blossom,
if not endless blue heavens in lament,

sweetness falling into earthen dust,
nothing left to bloom in other times?

5

I worry footsteps may damage earth,
injure roots beneath flowering trees,

but heaven can't understand, it's cut
and scattered child and grandchild.

Weighted branches lost a thousand
falling blossoms. Not one flourished.

Who calls this a home for the living?
Spring colors never entered the gate.

6

Branch after branch, bitter cold frost
comes like little knives killing spring.

Once the scattering ends, every tree's
heart is a mountain hollow howling

empty howls. All flurried color fallen,
petals fleck the ground like lit oil,

and it's clear: all heaven-and-earth's
ten thousand things unravel with ease.

7

Spring unfulfilled, come to nothing, I
weep, tears trailing out a dozen scars.

Lost blossoms bring butterfly flurries,
but a lost child leaves this old man

weaker still. If you're lifeless living,
you're the face of death death-infused.

What celestial phoenix carries prayers,
and who can knock at heaven's gate?

8

Calamity infecting a child is natural:
blossoms mostly fail. Still, I gather

ruins of the heart, a spent old man
cradling love's debris in endless night.

What can be said once sound dies away?
And once hope's dead, song's useless.

Old and sick – no child, no grandchild,
I stand like bundled firewood, alone.

9

Its ruin of pink blossoms seemingly
over, frost cut a last few dozen free

on breezes sighing: mouths of fish
nibbling at air over a shallow river.

Frozen tears never thaw, and no one
outlasts grief this bitter. Nothing left

here but empty shadows of lost days,
a little window of words is too large.

HEARTSONG

1

Autumn's lament for the ten thousand things,
these startling winds incite the timeless Way,

and climbing this hill renews such longing,
cold rains wounding the hundred grasses.

Those I love were always close, but in this
riot of scattering leaves, all that nurture's

gone. These five feelings already wounded,
how will I even die a death capable of itself?

2

These mornings on Lo-yang hilltops, I find
heaven boundless at the edge of sight. All

things return to the Great Transformation.
The six-dragon sun founders west into empty

wastelands. Every day now, it's more wolves,
more frost blanketing the grasses and trees,

and in this year all hunger, no grain left,
the birds are leaving these empty fields.

Whose child am I, standing beside some road
far from my old village, hair gone white?

I look bitterly at ever-green pine and cypress,
gaze up, accusing vast blue skies. The Way

never returns. It's all leaving and leaving,
appearance itself a grieving wound of hunger.

3

Unable to sleep, I pace back and forth.
So much bitter sorrow keeps me restless,

and deep in the night, I climb a tower,
remember long-ago stars and planets.

The four seasons turn. But will spring
renew the ten thousand things now?

They starved on Shou-yang Mountain
in protest: still no end to that farewell.

4

Great spirits kindred to heaven's Way,
who eats ferns on Shou-yang Mountain

now? It's all leaving and leaving, deep
outland distances. Sinking into the west,

the sun's six-dragon chariot returns home
again, the four seas ablaze with borrowed

light. Clear to the edge of sight, desolate
silence. A startling wind scatters things

away. Owls calling, haunting the treetops,
all those cowering birds huddle together.

There's a man alone out in these eastern
regions, a man at year's end forever grief-

stricken and hungry. A home needs guests
visiting at ease. How is it then, how is it

there's such joy in this poverty, content
enough now closing my brushwood gate?

5

A silver moon drifts among clouds on fire,
incandescent. Its ache of bright, mid-month

incandescence rivals broad daylight, pure
clarity confusing wise and foolish alike.

All transformation, the four seasons change,
and heaven's Way exhausts empty and full.

I've long dreaded today's already vanishing
moon, though it always returns to life again.

6

How can we meet on river bridges now,
how talk across boundless grasslands?

When the Han came splintering apart,
Wang Ts'an left for savage southlands,

and in silent outland depths, mourning
winds inciting such empty mountains,

I gaze up into these planets and stars,
wondering when I'll return. Long ago,

those I love scattered, body and spirit
going their separate ways. That farewell

between life and death still hasn't come,
but it's haunted my eyes forever now.

AUTUMN THOUGHTS

1

Lonely bones can't sleep nights. Singing
insects keep calling them, calling them.

And the old have no tears. When they sob,
autumn weeps dewdrops. Strength failing

all at once, as if cut loose, and ravages
everywhere, like weaving unraveled,

I touch thread-ends. No new feelings.
Memories crowding thickening sorrow,

how could I bear southbound sails, how
wander rivers and mountains of the past?

2

Under this autumn moon's face of frozen
beauty, the spirit driving an old wanderer

thins away. Cold dewdrops fall shattering
dreams. Biting winds comb cold through

bones. The sleeping-mat stamped with my
seal of sickness, whorled grief twisting,

there's nothing to depend on against fears.
Empty, sounds beginning nowhere, I listen.

Wu-t'ung trees, bare and majestic, sing
sound and echo clear as a *ch'in's* lament.

3

Moonlight edging through an empty
door, cold and valiant as sword-flight,

startled old bones sit dazed, suddenly
sicker and weaker still. Mourning

insects long for its piercing beauty.
Birds nest high, risking all its light.

A lovely widow's arranging old silks,
sobbing alone. It drags up memories,

but I can't retrace the phantom years.
Frail steps always return home at dusk.

4

Autumn's here. I'm old and poorer still,
not even a door in this tumbledown house.

A sliver of moonlight cast across the bed,
walls letting wind cut through clothes,

the furthest dreams never take me far,
and my frail heart returns home easily.

Year-end blossoms abandon late greens,
weaving lost splendor into rival swirls,

and in my sick worry, dazed by things,
country walks grow rare. O isolate beauty,

crickets hidden among grasses and roots,
your sense of life grown faint as my own.

5

Bamboo ticking in wind speaks. In dark
isolate rooms, I listen. Demons and gods

fill my frail ears, so blurred and faint I
can't tell them apart. Year-end leaves,

dry rain falling, scatter. Autumn clothes
thin cloud, my sick bones slice through

things clean. Though my bitter chant
still makes a poem, I'm withering autumn

ruin, strength following twilight away.
Trailed out, this fluttering thread of life:

no use saying it's tethered to the very
source of earth's life-bringing change.

6

Old bones fear the autumn moon. Autumn
moon, its swordblade of light – a chill

spirit sits frozen, and helpless against
even a sliver of its light. Widowed birds

build nests for it – blank mirror, drifting
ice bathed in winds of eternity. Afraid

my footsteps may startle away, sickness
vast, I can't brave ice. Waking into this

pure glistening light, I lie in bed alone,
emaciate and all fear, all heart of fear:

it rinses rivers so clean water vanishes,
renders foul and muddy clear and pure.

When strong, my poems were empty talk.
Now they're so frail, what is there to trust?

7

Countless strange worries. Old and sick,
a mind's not the same morning to night,

and autumn insects mourn a failing year,
sobbing tangled echoes I can't fathom.

My hair thin as autumn grass, a distant
scent moors me to chrysanthemum golds,

but light hurries easily into shadow now,
so how long can this late freshening last?

It's pointless to regret learning so little.
What good is knowledge against twilight?

Once my talent became clear, their spite
began, so wisdom born of solitude grew

deep early. *Guard depth, not appearance:*
isn't that what the ancients all taught?

8

Year's end in a dry world, autumn wind
starts-up all that arms-and-armor clatter.

Crickets working at song weave no cloth,
and when insects call and call for nothing,

autumn sounds sharpening past midnight,
feeble legs can't go any further. Once cut,

my black hair is like a garden in autumn:
it never grows back. And childhood's some

starveling blossom: brightness glimpsed,
never to return. Firm as mountain peaks,

the noble endure. Others bicker over trifles,
threads and feathers. The more they fight,

the more life they lose. The Way of heaven
warns against fullness: it just empties away.

9

Cold dew so rich in tired disappointment,
bare wind lush with sighs and whispers,

it's deep autumn: the bitter moon pure,
old insects singing their unworried songs.

Red pearls strung branch after branch,
lazy chrysanthemum golds everywhere:

these flowers and trees answer the season,
their cold splendor like another spring.

I mourn life scattering. So much here,
and is anything like this heart of mine?

10

Old, never the same person morning to night,
I pass days balanced between life and death,

sit full of repose after a single sip of wine.
Lying among ten thousand views, emptiness

itself, I can't even see out to the front gate,
and how can such ragged hearing trace wind?

Returned like pure form pared and whittled
away, I'm free of the least insight. And though

all my beginnings ended in tears, I'm happy
back home here in moonlit purity at death.

Alone, far from writer friends, I've grown
close to old outland hermits. Here, another

green year turning yellow sad enough, all
trace of autumn has already scattered away,

but the seasons crowd each other on, and if
ten thousand worries gather, it's only natural.

I once lived at ease among southern waters.
Now, it's poverty in rocky northlands, old

memories drowned in distant rivers, frail
thoughts tethered to Sung Mountain autumn.

I work a garden here, but never eat my fill,
and woodland clothes make an eyesore of me.

This thread of dust will never mend itself,
and who'll understand these ancient songs

now demons and gods wail in bamboo mystery,
now sharp swords fade into young dragons?

A depraved heart at the source of fate, life's
resolve brings many strange feelings now.

I always knew writing meant shabby clothes,
and yet, here I am at death – still a child

beginning, studying music, not that noise
making deafened fools of us. Words all light,

all incandescence of the heart – I wanted to
write them into stately peaks and summits.

11

My sudden flash of turning seasons ending,
everything broken and withered calls to me.

Bitter winds sob among thorn-date branches,
wu-t'ung leaves now faces of frost on high,

and as old insects cry parched-iron cries,
a startled animal howls lone, jade-pure howls.

Autumn air rinses sound, thinning it away,
and shadows hurry late light into exhaustion.

Things heard coalesce. You can't stop them,
can't flee what chokes the spirit. Too frail,

I walk among worry's scattered remains:
if I sit alone, who'll keep me company now,

not a thread of strength left, and this cut
longing filling ten hundred dagger-pints?

Hsieh T'iao's lucid poems, old T'ao Ch'ien's
gold chrysanthemums – leavings of long ago

gather and gather. Cast against all that, our
time's slight as a feather. And this isolate

mystery's alone here, year-end words another
leaf-fall I can't hold back scattering away.

NOTES

Mourning Lu Yin
10 of 10 sections

Page 3   *Lu Yin:* a minor poet and friend of Meng Chiao's.

Page 8   *Han Yü:* One of the great T'ang writers and a very close
friend of Meng Chiao's (see Introduction), Han Yü wrote
Lu Yin's epitaph because they were related.
Inkstick: Chinese writing ink is produced in small, dry
sticks. Before writing with a brush, a poet would rub an
inkstick on a wet inkstone to produce black ink – a kind
of meditative ritual.

Page 10   *Ancient sage of backalleys:* Yen Hui, Confucius' favorite dis-
ciple, is described in *Analects* 6/11 as living a life of en-
lightened poverty in a meager alley.
Lu Mountain recluse: This could be any of a number of
ancient recluses, though commentators identify him as a
near-contemporary of Meng Chiao: Yüan Lu-shan (Yüan
Te-hsiu, d. 754), who served as magistrate at Lu Moun-
tain, where he lived the most spartan of lives as he wisely
governed the impoverished people.

Page 14   *Banished immortals:* Li Po, the great T'ang poet, was the
most famous of these "banished immortals."

Cold Creek
8 of 8 sections

Page 18   *Heaven:* In ancient China, heaven meant "sky, fate, des-
tiny, etc.," but also "nature" and "natural process."
Evens all things out: A central, recurring concept in this se-
quence, drawn from the second chapter of the *Chuang
Tzu:* "On Evening Things Out." For Chuang-tzu, "eve-
ning things out" means to see the essential oneness of all
things, to "leap into the boundless and make it your
home" by embracing things directly, rather than being

trapped in one's intellectual distinctions and categories. After speaking of how limited such a life of distinctions is, he says, "Therefore the sage does not proceed in such a way, but illuminates all in the light of heaven."

Page 21   *Dragon:* As benevolent as it is destructive, the Chinese dragon is both feared and revered as the awesome force of life itself. Being the embodiment of *yang*, the dragon animates all things and is in constant transformation. It descends into deep waters in autumn, where it hibernates until spring, when it rises. As the dragon embodies the spirit of change, its awakening is equivelent to the awakening of spring and the return of life to earth.
Emperor Yao: mythic ruler (regnet 2357–2255 B.C.) during the legendary golden age of China.

Page 23   *Ch'i:* universal breath or life-giving principle.

Laments of the Gorges
10 of 10 sections

Page 27   *Gorges:* A two-hundred-mile stretch of very narrow canyons formed where the Yangtze River cuts through the Wu Mountains. Also called Three Gorges, as in the third section of this poem, because there are three distinct gorges. These dangerous canyons were located on the very outskirts of the civilized world, in a part of south China inhabited primarily by aboriginal peoples, and exiled scholar-officials often traveled downriver through them. They are famous in Chinese poetry (notably, Tu Fu's late work) for the river's violence and the towering cliffs alive with shrieking gibbons.

Page 34   *Kao Yao:* China's legendary first Minister of Justice (d. 2204 B.C.).

Page 35   *Ch'in:* ancient stringed instrument, which Chinese poets used to accompany the chanting of their poems. It is ancestor to the more familiar Japanese *koto.*
Spirit drifts high in the moon: The spirit is made up of *yin* and *yang* aspects. The moon is the heavenly incarnation of, is indeed the embryonic essence of, the *yin* spirit (sun being the source of *yang* spirit).

Page 39 *Death-owl's call:* The owl's voice resembles that of a ghost or spirit, so when it calls, it is thought to be calling the spirit of a dying person away.

Apricots Died Young
9 of 9 sections

Heartsong
6 of 8 sections

Page 57 *Shou-Yang Mountain:* When the Shang Dynasty was overthrown by the Chou Dynasty, Po Yi and Shu Ch'i (12th-c. B.C.) retired to Shou-yang Mountain in protest. Refusing to eat the grain of Chou, they lived on ferns until they finally died of cold and hunger.

Page 60 *Wang Ts'an:* To escape turmoil at the end of the Han Dynasty, the poet Wang Ts'an (A.D. 177–217) fled from the capital, Ch'ang-an, to southern China, which was inhabited by aboriginal people. He wandered there for many years.
Body and spirit: It was generally thought that the spirit leaves the body when a person dies or is terribly frightened.

Autumn Thoughts
11 of 15 sections

Page 66 *Dreams . . . :* It was also widely believed that the spirit could leave the body during sleep.

Page 69 *Chrysanthemum:* A favorite among Chinese poets, this flower blooms in autumn. Not coincidentally, it was popularly believed to promote longevity, so people drank infusions (especially wine) made with its petals.

Page 74 *Hsieh T'iao:* 5th-c. poet remembered for his landscape poems.
T'ao Ch'ien: One of China's greatest poets, T'ao Ch'ien (A.D. 365–427) is closely associated with chrysanthemums, which appear in several of his most famous passages.

FINDING LIST

Texts

1. *Meng Tung-yeh shih-chu.* Hua Ch'en-chih, ed. (Page number).
2. *Meng Tung-yeh chi.* SPPY. (*Chüan* and page number).
3. *Meng Tung-yeh shih-chu.* Ch'en Yen-chien, ed. and comm. (*Chüan* and page number).

Page	1. *Meng Tung-yeh shih-chi*	2. *Meng Tung-yeh chi*	3. *Meng Tung-yeh shih-chu*
3	190	10.7b	10.10a
15	88	5.6b	5.8b
27	185	10.4b	10.6a
41	187	10.6a	10.8b
53	33	2.6a	2.8b
61	58	4.1a	4.1a

FURTHER READING

Graham, A. C. *Poems of the Late T'ang* (Penguin, 1965). (This anthology summarizes the alternative mid-T'ang tradition which Meng Chiao did so much to initiate: late Tu Fu, Meng Chiao, Han Yü, Lu T'ung, Li Ho, Tu Mu, Li Shang-yin.)

Neinhauser, William, ed. *The Indiana Companion to Traditional Chinese Literature* (Indiana University Press, 1986).

Owen, Stephen. *The Poetry of Meng Chiao and Han Yü* (Yale University Press, 1975).

George Seferis: Collected Poems (1924–1955), translated, edited, and introduced by Edmund Keeley and Philip Sherrard

Collected Poems of Lucio Piccolo, translated and edited by Brian Swann and Ruth Feldman

C. P. Cavafy: Collected Poems, translated by Edmund Keeley and Philip Sherrard and edited by George Savidis

Benny Andersen: Selected Poems, translated by Alexander Taylor

Selected Poetry of Andrea Zanzotto, edited and translated by Ruth Feldman and Brian Swann

Poems of René Char, translated and annnotated by Mary Ann Caws and Jonathan Griffin

Selected Poems of Tudor Arghezi, translated by Michale Impey and Brian Swann

"The Survivor" and Other Poems by Tadeusz Różewicz, translated and introduced by Magnus J. Krynski and Robert A. Maguire

"Harsh World" and Other Poems by Angel González, translated by Donald D. Walsh

Ritsos in Parentheses, translations and introduction by Edmund Keeley

Salamander: Selected Poems of Robert Marteau, translated by Anne Winters

Angelos Sikelianos: Selected Poems, translated and introduced by Edmund Keeley and Philip Sherrard

Dante's "Rime," translated by Patrick Diehl

Selected Later Poems of Marie Luise Kashnitz, translated by Lisel Mueller

Osip Mandelstam's "Stone," translated and introduced by Robert Tracy

The Dawn Is Always New: Selected Poetry of Rocco Scotellaro, translated by Ruth Feldman and Brian Swann

Sounds, Feelings, Thoughts: Seventy Poems by Wisława Szymborska, translated and introduced by Magnus J. Krynski and Robert A. Maguire

The Man I Pretend to Be: "The Colloquies" and Selected Poems of Guido Gozzano, translated and edited by Michael Palma, with an introductory essay by Eugenio Montale

D'Après Tout: Poems by Jean Follain, translated by Heather McHugh

Songs of Something Else: Selected Poems of Gunnar Ekelöf, translated by Leonard Nathan and James Larson

The Little Treasury of One Hundred People, One Poem Each, compiled by Fujiwara No Sadaie and translated by Tom Galt

The Ellipse: Selected Poems of Leonardo Sinisgalli, translated by W. S. Di Piero

The Difficult Days by Roberto Sosa, translated by Jim Lindsey

Hymns and Fragments by Friedrich Hölderlin, translated and introduced by Richard Sieburth

The Silence Afterwards: Selected Poems of Rolf Jacobsen, translated and edited by Roger Greenwald

Rilke: Between Roots, selected poems rendered from the German by Rika Lesser

In the Storm of Roses: Selected Poems by Ingeborg Bachmann, translated, edited, and introduced by Mark Anderson

Birds and Other Relations: Selected Poetry of Dezső Tandori, translated by Bruce Berlind

Brocade River Poems: Selected Works of the Tang Dynasty Courtesan Xue Tao, translated and introduced by Jeanne Larsen

The True Subject: Selected Poems of Faiz Ahmed Faiz, translated by Naomi Lazard

My Name on the Wind: Selected Poems of Diego Valeri, translated by Michael Palma

Aeschylus: The Suppliants, translated by Peter Burian

Foamy Sky: The Major Poems of Miklós Radnóti, selected and translated by Zsuzsanna Ozsváth and Frederick Turner

La Fontaine's Bawdy: Of Libertines, Louts, and Lechers, translated by Norman R. Shapiro

A Child Is Not a Knife: Selected Poems of Göran Sonnevi, translated and edited by Rika Lesser

George Seferis: Collected Poems, Revised Edition, translated, edited, and introduced by Edmund Keeley and Philip Sherrard

C. P. Cavafy: Collected Poems, Revised Edition, translated and introduced by Edmund Keeley and Philip Sherrard, edited by George Savidis

The Late Poems of Meng Chiao, translated by David Hinton
Leopardi: Selected Poems, translated and introduced by Eamon Grennan

9 780691 012360